Mary Deioma

Copyright - © 2014 Mary Deioma

Sign up to receive a free newsletter.

lovedatranscendentjourney.com

Loved: A Transcendent Journey

Copyright - © 2014 Mary Deioma
All rights reserved. No part of this book may be used, transmitted, or reproduced in any manner whatsoever, without written permission from the author.

The author of this of this book makes no claims for its use. This information is not meant to treat, diagnose, advise or cure any illness. The author of this book does not dispense any medical advice or prescribe the use of any technique as a form of treatment for physical or emotional problems. In the event that you use any information in this book, the author assumes no responsibility for your actions.

First Edition

ISBN-13: 978-1495934612
ISBN-10: 1495934616

In Gratitude vii

1 ∞ From Great Heights 1

2 ∞ Would Smell as Sweet 5

3 ∞ From the Depths to Hope 9

4 ∞ Proof for God 11

5 ∞ Life Review 15

6 ∞ Early Days 17

7 ∞ Reading 23

8 ∞ Time Travel 27

9 ∞ Health 31

10 ∞ Ineffable 33

11 ∞ The Heart 35

12 ∞ Enlightenment 37

13 ∞ Now What? 61

14 ∞ Oneself 67

15 ∞ What About...? 71

16 ∞ Return to the Vast Void	77
17 ∞ Pause Before the Gate of Hell	79
18 ∞ Neither Here Nor There	81
19 ∞ I'm Going Back In	85
20 ∞ Suffering: Good and Evil	93
21 ∞ Heaven's Heavens	97
22 ∞ Super States	101
23 ∞ Visitation	105
24 ∞ Out-of-body Experiences	109
25 ∞ Prophecy	115
26 ∞ Past Lives	119
27 ∞ Confessions of a Doomtard	123
28 ∞ Unfolding the Experience	127
29 ∞ Why Me?	131
30 ∞ Thoughts	135
Helpful Books	I

In Gratitude

This book would not be in existence without the efforts, contributions and unconditional love of many people who really are masters each in their own signature way.

I am forever grateful from the deepest regions of my heart, for my very dear friend Kathleen Lammens. Her exclamation upon hearing my story - "This has to be a movie!" - set me on a new course. I began to think about making my story available to a wider audience than just my closest friends and family. She is also the one who cajoled me into going to my first International Association for Near Death Studies (IANDS) meeting in Orange County (OC). Kathy also contributed to the editing and helped me to sort out the most important stories to share.

My deep abiding love for my amazing, literal genius of a big sister. She believes me and in me! She is my mentor and spiritual guide for this whole lifetime. She is my database of all information, especially what should "go without saying," because for me, it rarely does. She slogged through every sentence with me - adding her finesse here and there - since grammar and punctuation are two of those things that don't go without saying. Is there a greater word than grateful? That is how I feel for Kayte Deioma.

I am grateful to my brother Bob, AKA Robert Deioma, AKA the multitalented Bubba Da Skitso. He is my personal comedian and deep belly laugh generator. He is also one of the greatest healers with humor. I feel privileged to be his sister and friend.

To my Mom and Dad who gave me this opportunity to play in this physical playground, "Thank you!"

I am so thankful to Mark Piatelli for his contributions to this project and our mastermind group. He turned out to be my key to accessing such a deep place of trust, that I released my fear of public speaking. This gift came miraculously - just in time - before I was to speak to my first large crowd!

I am grateful to Juanita Catlett for being the first to hear and believe.

Many thanks to my friends and sojourners, Angel Mundt Baker and Caren Frances, for their spiritual support and encouragement.

I am so grateful to OC IANDS and LA IANDS and especially, Denis Purcell, Steve Damroth, Bob Siress, Lee Offenhauer, Carolyn Whittaker, Angel Powers and Robin Barr! IANDS created a safe haven to share with people who are open, interested, loving and understand when I say "You know what I am saying?"

I have tremendous gratitude to Chuck Swedrock and Susan Amsden for inviting me to speak at Tucson IANDS and encouraging me to get going with writing.

I feel wonderfully blessed to consider as my friends the many NDEers, Beverly Brodsky, Deirdre Dewitt Maltby, Claudia

Edge, Rudy "Rudenski", Dottie Clark and Ellyn Dye. I feel we are all part of a kindred soul group!

I am also grateful those who provide the fuel so that I am able attain lift off....

1 ∞ From Great Heights

Suddenly I was gripped with terror. It came out of nowhere, and for no obvious reason. I was at a carnival with my friend, and we were waiting in line for a ride that I loved! I was not remotely afraid of this ride. I was confused as to why I was suddenly gripped with terror! It felt like two straps wrapped around my torso like a vice. I was startled because I personally did not have any reason to feel fear in that moment. However, the pressing terror was unmistakably tangible. On autopilot my eyes immediately began to scan the crowd. Off in the distance my gaze landed on a bungee jumper ride. I knew for certain that the girl at the top was not going to jump. It clicked inside me that the terror gripping me was hers and she was "Not gonna! Not gonna!"

I said to my friend "Do you see that bungee jumper ride? That girl is not going to jump." First my friend asked, "How do you know it is a girl, it's too far to tell. And how do you know she is not going to jump? She has to jump at the end of the countdown." We paused to listen to the countdown and we could hear it faintly in the distance 5, 4, 3, 2, 1....... She didn't jump. My friend turned in amazement. How did you know?!!! I just knew. I couldn't say how at that point, still gripped with this vice of terror; I only shrugged to say I don't know. As we continued to watch, the ride operator walked over to the girl and said something. I perceived this cord of light that seemed to droop with weight across the distance between the bungee jumper and me, connecting us. I then felt the invisible cord that was connecting us was cut, and the vise-like grip on my torso was released. I then felt a valve-like lever was opened at the bottom of my feet, and a gush of what felt like water was released out the bottom of my feet into the earth below. I no longer felt the connection, or the terror, or any knowing about her or her feelings. I then thought she would jump, but this time I wasn't certain. I no longer had any additional information. I felt only curious about what she would do next.

Count down. As her body began to move, I could tell she had turned around. So instead of going forward off of the platform, she allowed herself to gently fall backwards off of the platform. As she reached the length of the rope, it safely and smoothly caught her descent and swung gently to a stop. She appeared jubilant! Arms pumping in triumph!.....

Something very real had just happened to me. I could not deny it to myself anymore. Just what it was that happened or why, I did not yet know. As I thought about it later, there was no question in my mind that I had felt that girl's emotions. But why and how? Was it some survival instinct left over from when we were cave dwellers and needed to contact others in times of crisis over vast distances? Was it some radar signal from one brain to the next? If so, how did that signal propagate from one point to the next. Did my participation in her experience help her any? Did it benefit me? Why did I seem to be the only one who could perceive it? Was I psychic? What is psychic? How does that operate? What was the cord about? And what about all the other sensations and emotions, and how and what is "just knowing?" Lots of questions arose, with no immediate answers.

2 ∞ Would Smell as Sweet

People generally accept we have 5 senses - sight, smell, taste, touch and hearing. But in reality we all have many more than 5 senses and more than 5 sensory organs.

Recently there have been studies about humans' ability to sense pheromones, creating a chemical and hormonal reaction within us. In America, our entire society - including me - has been influenced by advertisers, into using deodorant and antiperspirant. They have placed a negative value on the odor that naturally emanates from our bodies. In other cultures, the natural odors are valued as desirable and attractive. By blocking odor and pheromone emissions we may have impaired the mating process - not improved upon it. Sadly we have lost this added dimension of reality. This data which might formerly have been useful to us, has been removed from our experience.

Even among the more generally accepted senses, we can observe that individuals have differing degrees of discernment. People have unique preferences and biological reactions to smells; perfume testers have extraordinary sensitivity in this area. We all have different taste buds and preferences to salty, sour, sweet, spicy, savory, bitter and bland; chefs and food flavor developers must have very highly developed palates.

Many factors impact our senses. There is even variance of experience within the same individual. Perhaps you have lost the sense of smell or taste during a cold. Certain chemicals increase our sensory acuity, as do emotion and hunger.

Many people around the world believe we have additional senses reflected in language like "I feel it in my bones," or a "gut feeling." We also must acknowledge that even animals have different senses to detect fear, danger, or food safety.

If I can't smell fear, do I deny that smelling fear is possible? Take for example a color blind person who insists that in reality there is no such thing as color. They believe the rest of the world is deluding themselves and imagining color. That doesn't negate your experience of colorful reality. You perceive a dimension that they do not. One person's - or even billions of people's - lack of, or denial of a perception, does not invalidate the data. So consider that the deepest, most dimensional experience of reality - even if it has not yet been your experience - may be the truest.

People are usually limited to their own perception of reality information. Over time, I have come to perceive not only my own direct experience of reality data but also the energy of God, angels and spirits, the information of the future, plants, animals and earth. I understand that all are connected to each other and to us. I also empathically perceive emotional data. This I perceive as real information that exists. I too used to have my access to this information filtered by my denial of its existence. What follows is the journey that changed my perspective and opened me up to a greater reality.

3 ∞ From the Depths to Hope

I had long since put the mystery of the bungee jumper to the back of my mind. I totally forgot about it for a while.

I experienced a long phase of bad luck that convinced me that there must not be a God. I lost my college funding, which forced me to move and give away my beloved cat. Then I lost my job and had to relocate to a new city to find work. I ended up renting a room in a house with 3 people I didn't know.

So there I was feeling all alone. It was New Year's Eve, and I was in a room with no furniture, sleeping on the floor and feeling miserable. From my skeptical state of doubting God's existence, I decided to test God.

I prayed with all my might for the most unlikely wish. I prayed that I would get a New Year's kiss. It was only a few hours from midnight. I felt like an ugly loser. I curled up in my sleeping bag on the floor in a dark empty room in a town where I didn't know a single soul. I drifted off to sleep for a nap at about 6pm.

Around 7pm there was a knock on my door. It was one of my new roommates who said a group was going to a local bar for New Year's celebration and wanted to know if I wanted to come along. I did go out and, completely unexpectedly, I did receive a very wonderful kiss at the stroke of midnight that New Year. This qualified as a true miracle for me. I still was not completely convinced God existed, but now I had this idea of testing for proof of God.

4 ∞ Proof for God

It occurred to me that, if there is a God, there should be a way to prove it, or to find evidence of God, that is significant, verifiable, repeatable and shareable. Isn't that is what science is looking for? If something is really there, we should be able to find it.

A "proof" in math - from what I remembered - states a hypothesis, starting with an assumption that the hypothesis is correct. Then states assumptions as "givens," and concludes with an "If this is true, then that consequence is true" statement called a theorem. Then you design an experiment or way to test it.

Hypothesis - God is real and exists.

Given, God is real > then it is possible that some accounts of God (like in the Bible) are real.

If some accounts are real, then humans had everything necessary to experience God 5000 or so years ago.

Also given that, as far as I know, humans have not changed very much in 5000 years.

If God is real and humans had everything necessary to experience God, and I am reasonably similar to early humans, then it is possible for me (and any humans today) to experience God.

It didn't make sense to me that if there is a God, God would have only spoken to ancient people.

Then it occurred to me to look at the Near Death Experience (NDE) as a template for how to proceed with my own direct contact with the Divine. I certainly didn't want to actually die to experience God, but in the near death experiences, one of the things that they often mention is a life review. I have only read a couple of dozen accounts, but I highly recommend it. I believe just reading them has a direct effect on the reader.

5 ∞ Life Review

Many near death experiences speak about the life review being instantaneous, panoramic and holographic or 3 dimensional and I thought, "Well, I may not be able to replicate that, but what I can do is I can think about my own life." So I set about doing just that, a life review. I gave myself a lot more time than they typically report which is pretty instantaneous. I thought, "It takes as long as it takes."

I started at my earliest year that I could remember. I tried to remember something from every year, with as much detail as I could fill in. To jog my memory I considered what type of experiences might be especially memorable for someone of each age. Did I remember learning to ride a bike? Did I remember the first time I could reach the faucet by myself?

Did I remember the first time I could reach the light switch? Or could I remember the first time I could reach the top of the door frame? Did I remember my first teachers or my first love or my first kiss? What were the good events, and what were the bad events? I just kept asking myself, "What else can I remember?" And then I considered if there were lessons to learn from every event that I could remember, and contemplated what they were about. What was the value of each experience? Was there something to learn? What might the other people have been feeling?

6 ∞ Early Days

On the surface, my life may have seemed ideal. In reality, although there were many good moments, my inner life was challenging. I was the fifth of eight children. Our family self-organized into the 4 big kids and the 4 little kids, and I was the "biggest little kid." There were five girls and three boys. I was sandwiched between boys as the birth order was two girls, two boys, one girl (me), one boy and two more girls. My mom use to say, "One child takes all your time. More than one can't take more than all your time." The up-side of lots of siblings is there is usually someone to play with, when you are getting along. The down-side is never getting enough of mom and dad's attention. Not that you know what the issue is, because you just grow up thinking that is the way it is for everyone. I was probably pretty well cared for the first nine months. When I was born in the spring, our family of seven (so far) lived in a small cottage by a lake.

In doing the life review process I remembered being an infant, preverbal, probably only weeks old. I was in my grandfather's arms and feeling his love. I looked out over water, and as I looked, the horizon gently swayed. I heard the water gently lapping against the small boat we were in. I saw where the water met the shore, and there was a bank of grass that led to a wall of thick trees all lined up. I could feel my grandfather's embrace and a cocoon of his love.

I shared this memory with my mom, and asked her if it was possible that this was a real memory. She did say that the only time my grandfather held me as an infant was when the family lived in the cottage by the lake, and there was a small boat. By summer we moved to the new house.

I continued my life review, and I remembered various events all throughout my life. I recalled some things that I regretted. I looked at the opportunity to learn in each of those experiences and tried to put myself in the other people's shoes for each event. I considered what they might have been feeling during those events. I proceeded to go through this process for the next several months.

I remembered when I was three or four, I used to see monsters in my bedroom at night. These beings that I saw when I was very young would be half in the shadows and half in my mind's eye. The only one I remember having put any kind of name to was something like a werewolf, but there were several different types, all very frightening.

Because of these experiences my mom took me to see the priest. The priest said to my mom "Children have very active imaginations." Then he bent down to talk to me and said, "Just repeat, 'There is no such thing as ghosts and eventually they will go away." Afterward, I remembered being in my bed with the covers up to my nose, peeking out and seeing the werewolf and repeating "There is no such thing as ghosts" out loud. And after about the twentieth repetition, he got sucked away into oblivion and disappeared. After that I was not bothered so much by monsters.

My mom was a huge influence in my spiritual life, of course, but not with her religious beliefs. It was little tricks here and there that made the most impact in my spiritual evolution. She told me very early how to program my dreams. She said that before I go to bed, I should tell myself that I will remember my dreams, and I will wake up rested and refreshed. She also said I could ask for specific solutions, and I would dream answers.

Mom shared an effective technique for finding things. The patron saint of lost items is St Anthony. She taught me to pray, "Tony, Tony look around. Something's lost and must be found," and then pause and see what comes to mind. Often in that space after the question, an idea or image pops into my mind, and the exact location of the missing item is revealed.

I had gotten to about grade school in the memory process. I remembered in the Catholic school where I went to school, we were taught that the priests and the nuns were intermediaries to God. But I never accepted that. It never seemed plausible that they had any greater access to God than anyone else. Only a few times did I question and challenge their perspective. I remember questioning why does Jesus have brothers and sisters in the Bible and the Catholic position then was that Jesus is an only child of an eternal virgin? I never got a straight answer on that one.

I also felt they were not interpreting the meaning of the Bible correctly. This led me to flat out reject whatever else they were trying to say. I just quietly went my own way. The distinct memory that surfaced around this time period was that I had wanted to be a spiritual leader and do it right. This desire had never been expressed out loud before, not even to myself. In my life review, I remembered being in church with my family. The 10 of us took up a whole pew. I imagined being chosen by God, a ray of light coming in through the stained glass windows and shining only on me.

In my present life, the surfacing of this memory had an instant effect and literally changed the course of my life. I instantly felt like a had found a missing part of my soul. The desire felt so authentic, like I have excavated part of the treasure of who I really am. The day that I remembered my secret desire was a Saturday and I worked a half day with one co-worker and I shared this desire out loud for the first time, and I also shared I was having this wonderful warm blanket enveloping me feeling. I thought it might be an Angel.

That afternoon I after work I felt pulled to go to a bookstore and in the discount section there were six spiritual books calling my name, so to speak. I don't remember now what all the books were, but one of them was the Dead Sea Scrolls.

Continuing with the life review, I remembered a wonderful experience on the last day of eighth grade. I went to the playground after school and climbed the monkey bars and sat on the top thinking about the future and my future-self. Suddenly, I had this expansive moment where it felt like many of my future selves were looking back through time to that moment, just like I am doing right now as I write this. And each time I remember that moment, that girl in the past is feeling the connection through time, in the eternal present moment.

7 ∞ Reading

At the same time, I was doing the life review, I implemented the practice of reading every single night. I set aside about 20 minutes each night to read something spiritual. I started with the Bible. I had so many questions about it. During this time, I began a sort of dialog with God and Angels as part of the experiment. I was throwing out challenges for proof and asking a lot of questions. I just started with a few, but eventually it became almost a constant discussion in my head. In the back of my mind, as I was doing this life review thing, I got a message from spirit saying to "PREPARE." So I understood that doing this life review process and reading 20 minutes a day was preparing me for something, but exactly for what I was not sure.

I had never read the Bible all the way through, even with 12 years of Catholic school, so I now decided to give it a read. It turned out to be a very good thing to read the Bible, even though I still don't think of it as being wholly literal. I look at it as guidance that may or may not speak to me at any given time. Let's just say it is a "good" book. I think there is a lot of information there, but it is definitely important to consider the culture and context in which it was written and promoted.

During one of the times I was reading the Bible, in my mind I was asking for proof. I was reading in the living room of the apartment. One of my roommates was on the balcony with the door open, facing back into the room. The whole room was quiet because I was reading. In my mind, I was asking for proof - proof of spirit, proof of God or whatever. Suddenly the tape player switched on all by itself! It never happened before and it never happened again. It seemed to respond specifically to my request.

Sometime later, I was living with a different roommate, and we both had cats. I was laying on my stomach reading, head toward the wall, and feet toward the door. Again I was asking for supernatural proof. Suddenly, and all at once, I heard her cat come running down the hallway, and I noticed my cat, who had been relaxed at my shoulder, tensed and fixed his eyes at the foot of the bed. I felt a presence there too. I slowly turned my head to see what was there, and I saw a human shaped smudge. Not dense enough to call a shadow, but like a very fine smoke or mist. I freaked out and felt extremely frightened! I said "Go away! I am not ready yet!" It went away immediately. Whew! That was certainly some convincing evidence. Even so, my mind still wanted to try to find ways to explain it away and forget about it.

On another visit to the bookstore I was walking down the aisle, not having found what I was looking for. I was striding pretty quickly since I had just decided to leave and I wasn't looking at the books anymore. As I was heading for the door, a book was launched from the shelf and landed in my hands! It was a big book too and heavy! I immediately went around to the other side of the bookcase to see if someone had thrown it or pushed it, but no one was there, and the bookcase did not go through to the other side. I looked down at the title of the book. I had never heard of it. It was the Nag Hammadi Library. I just could not explain the catapulting book away. Immediately the scene from the City of Angels movie with all the Angels in the library came to my mind.

Well, I did buy that book and I read it. There were a lot of words I still don't understand, but I kept at it. I did not know it then, but it had a powerful effect on me. The Nag Hammadi is part of the Gnostic texts. Some sections were written in the first century. They included some people's direct experience of God. That is why it is called gnosis because when you experience something, you no longer need to have faith about it, you come to a place of knowing it.

8 ∞ Time Travel

In the course of doing the life review process, I came to a period of my life which caused me great pain every single time I thought about it. I had been bullied terribly at school between the ages of 6 to 14 . I did not want to think about this time in my life, but I knew to be faithful to the process, I would have to. I began asking the question: Was there any value in these experiences? I realized that inventing different ways to prevent the bullying situation from happening helped me learn the skill of creative problem solving, which has had value in my life.

The next part of the process was even more difficult - to imagine it from his perspective. I don't think I was able to actually do that successfully. Where my mind would go - where it almost always went when I thought of these events -

was to wish wholeheartedly that I could go back in time and stop them before they ever happened. I really felt there was no possible way my soul would have chosen to experience those events, and I wished they just never had to happen. I have watched every single time travel movie, and every one of them made me feel in my heart that it was possible to go back in time. I just knew it very deep in my core that time travel must be possible.

One night around this part of the review process, I went to sleep as usual, but I woke up in my child-self body. I found myself to be around the age of 13 or 14. It took me a few seconds to get my bearings, and I suddenly realized the bully was approaching. Then I realized I was back in time! I thought, "Oh shit! I have no idea what to do!"

I did not actually believe this could happen to me, so I had no plan. I panicked for a second, looking for somewhere to hide, but there was nowhere to run. The only advantage I had compared to when I was a child, was that I had my adult mind, even though I was inside my child body. I thought to myself, "I will fight! And he will know, if nothing else, that he will also feel pain!" As he approached me, I launched myself at him and fought as hard as I could with every ounce of power I could bring to bear. I punched and kicked and scratched and bit. I felt the punches were causing the most pain, so then I just focused on that, really pummeling his arms and gut. I unleashed all the pent up anger I had for what he had done to me over the years. Aaaaugh! And mid-punch suddenly I was back in this time, in my bed, awake. I took a moment to get my bearings. Suddenly a flood of new memories flashed in my mind's eye and downloaded into my mind. Then I had two timelines of memories. I had the original timeline where I never fought back. I also had a second new timeline and new memories of the intervening years, from a life that unfolded as a result of fighting back. The first timeline is now fading a little bit, but it's still there.

That was a pretty profound experience for me. The person who returned to this time was a different person than the one who left. Before this time travel experience, I was the kind of person who did not make a scene. I wouldn't send a meal back if it was wrong. I didn't complain, or ever stand up for myself. The person who came back was bold. Now I was not going to take any grief from anyone. For a while I relished bad customer service because it gave me an opportunity to fight, to stand up for my rights.

Shortly after this I became so aggressive that I was fighting at work with my co-workers. I got called into the boss's office, and she told me very calmly that behavior was not acceptable. I realized how different I had become, and I needed to get some balance. It's OK to be assertive instead of a doormat, but there is no need to be aggressive. After the reprimand at work, I wasn't coping well and sought some help with a therapist. She helped me to vent some of that anger and helped me find some balance for a while, but the real healing of this childhood pain did not come until much later.

9 ∞ Health

One other thing helped set the stage for enlightenment.

I found out I had Celiac Disease, and I needed to change to a gluten free diet and eat a lot more vegetables. As a result, I became a lot healthier physically. I feel strongly that being healthier was a very important part of the preparation for enlightenment. I didn't really want to change my diet, but having a healthier body made my being more able to withstand the increased bandwidth of energy.

I still didn't know what I was waiting for, but I felt like I was preparing for something. I tried to read the signs.

10 ∞ Ineffable

I want to acknowledge at the outset that it's hard to put words to what is ineffable. By using words, it automatically limits the magnificence, intensity and grandeur of what this multi-dimensional experience is, to a limited construct within one's imagination. So it feels inadequate to me to actually do it, but right at this moment, I know of no other way available to me to share what it is that I experienced.

Concurrent with this challenge of ineffability, is my deep desire to connect through sharing. I feel that Divine Love wants the information to be known and wants it to be shared. Not to share would be more of a disservice.

Nevertheless, I feel frustrated that there are not enough words, or that the words I use have a complex meaning that includes connotations and double meanings that aren't part of what is intended.

There is an internal joy, an internal love that wants to be expressed, to lift others up and to love others.

11 ∞ The Heart

I met Faruque in 1993. For our first date we had a chaperone. Faruque was so adorable! The chaperone was his roommate and he was adorable too. I was not very experienced at dating myself, but the idea of a chaperone at 20-something, was so funny to me. I was amused and thought "I am just going to have fun and enjoy myself and see what happens." I drove, so at the end of the night I was dropping them off, and his roommate left us alone to talk in the car for a few minutes. Finally there came our moment, and we kissed, closed-lipped, just a peck on the lips. I think it must have been his first kiss. It was the sweetest kiss ever. My heart opened up right then, and I was never the same again. We had some wonderful times together. We never ran out of things to talk about. We became engaged a few years later. Then in 2000 he needed to go to

Bangladesh because his mother was in the hospital. I had a feeling that something terrible was going to happen to him during that trip, and I asked him not to go, but I knew he had to go for his mother. So I asked that he at least be careful.

12 ∞ Enlightenment

About 3 days before Faruque was set to return, I talked to him on the phone. He told me that in three days, when he returned, we would get married. I was very excited. It was one of the happiest days of my life. I went to bed and slept better than I ever slept before. I got up in the morning and I went to work.

It was just like any regular Thursday. I was singing as I drove in to work. "I got that joy, joy, joy, joy down in my heart....I'm so happy, so very happy.....and if the devil doesn't like it he can sit on a tack, ouch!......"

When I got to that part of the song, I felt like I had sat on a tack and felt a very painful pinch on my behind. It happened again on the next repetition and I thought "Whoa I better stop singing that song." I thought it ironic and kind of funny.

At work everything was pretty normal. Suddenly I was hit with these very severe menstrual cramps. The pain was so intense that I tipped my chair back and put my feet up on the desk to shift my center of gravity and try to take some of the pressure off. It was too deep a pain to do any more than take some pain relievers, breathe through it as best I could, and affirm that it would be over soon.

While in that position, my very unsympathetic boss, who was known for being very demanding and downright mean, walked by my cubicle. I was in no mood to be challenged at that time and I looked him straight in the eye and thought, "Go ahead and make my day, I dare you!" And whether it was the look I gave him or some other miracle, he said nothing and let me be.

Not too long after that I was feeling fine again when Faruque's roommate called me at work. His roommate had never called me before, let alone at work. I didn't know he even knew my phone number, or even knew where I worked. He seemed drunk. He just kept repeating "You're a smart girl. You're a smart girl."

I was angry he called me while he was drunk, at my place of work, for basically nothing. Moments after I hung up, I just suddenly knew... I felt as if I had been kicked really hard in the stomach (higher up than the cramps). I just knew Faruque was married. Even though his roommate never said the words, I understood that he was telling me that Faruque got married. I knew in my soul that it was the truth.

I didn't find out until years later that his roommate never even knew Faruque was married officially until Faruque got back from his trip to Bangladesh days later. So he didn't really say Faruque was married, and nobody else told me that Faruque was married, so how did I know he was? I just knew it to such an extent that I thought I had been told in so many words.

So there I was at work in my cubicle. I had just hung up the phone, knowing my fiancé had just married some arranged bride. Feeling kicked in the stomach, I hunched over for a few minutes in pain. I am not even sure if I felt the pain first, or had the knowing first. I was *completely devastated.* But I was at work, and I thought no way I am going to lose it at the office. So I just shut my emotions down. I imagined a vise gripping my torso. All the muscles in the center of me clamped down so that I couldn't feel anything. I was pretty numb, but I maintained anger at his roommate for calling me at work. That was the only emotion I could hang on to, so that I didn't fall apart. I kept thinking "I'm not gonna lose it."

The call happened around 10 o'clock in the morning, and I made it all the way until about 4pm. I was supposed to stay until 5 but I thought, "I'm out." As I was driving home, traffic was slow and steady. I had time to think.

In my mind, I am having a conversation with God. And I think, "OK, What am I going to do?" I remembered having read *The Seat of the Soul* by Gary Zukoff recently, and he said if you are having strong emotions, that is when you should feel them. You should not set them aside. When those emotions or situations come to the front, that is when you should feel them. So FEEL your emotions!

So I thought, OK, I am going to try to feel them. I'm just going to let it be as painful as it is. So I started to loosen up and relax my muscles so that I could actually feel the pain. And then the pain started full force! It skipped right past the point where I could cry, to a place too painful to even cry. I had never experienced that before. I was thinking my heart was literally damaged or breaking. I thought briefly that it might have been severe enough to pull the car over and call 911, but I was still mad.

I was angry and I was really thinking about the situation. I was more angry at God, IF there was a God (I was still not sure at this point). I thought, if there is a God, you totally suck! I felt betrayed, because I felt guided into that relationship. I knew we loved each other. I knew he loved me.

I also knew intellectually, but I didn't truly get it until that moment, the kind of pressure that his family was putting on him to be in an arranged marriage, rather than let him choose his own wife. I could understand that he was a human being, and that he had his faults and weaknesses. I loved him!

For that reason, my anger was directed at God. I thought God screwed me by even introducing us in the first place, and leading me down this path of destruction. It was really not right, just totally not right, and so I was pissed at God and I was feeling tremendous pain, searing physical and emotional pain, and I was devastated! This whole future I had planned just evaporated. Gone forever! Never gonna happen, none of it, EVER.

I had to figure out what to do. I thought, "What would Mother Theresa do in this situation?" I instantly knew Mother Theresa would say "love anyway." So I asked myself, "Can I love anyway? Yes, I can." So, I LOVED! I let the love feeling come into my heart. I felt, "I can love him even with his poor decision. I can love his family in spite of their terrible actions." I felt love in my heart for them even with the pain still there.

Then I wondered "What would Jesus do?" The instant answer was Jesus would say "Forgive your enemies." I asked "Can I forgive him? Can I forgive his family?" and I thought "Yeah, I can forgive his family." I had some small understanding of their justifications which led me to a place where I could forgive them. So I did that. I really meant it too, it wasn't just lip service. I saw that they live in a different world than I do. They have different values. What is important to them is not what is important to me. Yes, I decided, I can forgive them, allowing a feeling of forgiveness into my heart.

And then I thought, "What would Mohammed do?" They were Muslim, and I had been learning about Mohammed. Mohammed's main message is to submit. I used to think that meant to be humiliated, but suddenly in that moment, I understood it meant to turn your life over to God and release yourself.

I also saw it as if I was to turn my life IN to God like homework. As if to say "I've been doing the best I can. I did the best I could and this is where I'm at. I leave it in your hands God. I did my homework and now it is for you to grade." I imagined my heart going out of my chest and up to God. I unzipped my jacket and thought "Here, you take my pain too, I turn it all over to you, God."

What transpired next took place in real time of just a second and a half, but seemed completely outside of time.

Suddenly, a beam of *PURE WHITE* came out of the sky and came down to a point and touched me on my right shoulder, gently, tangibly, firmly and yet compassionately. As the beam approached, I had this sudden sense of recognition! "Oh Yeah! I remember! Of course! This is so basic and natural!

How could I have forgotten? I am you and you are me!!!!! I AM GOD!" Not at all the idea I had of God before this moment. I suddenly remembered WHO I AM! I am Divinity! I am love. The beam itself was a manifestation of God. That is God. I remembered that is who I am. I remembered, I am love and I am loved. The kind of love I felt was like a parent for their precious infant. I was being loved like a precious child. I was being loved deeply as an adorable, darling, baby!

As the beam descended, I saw the scene unfold from several perspectives. My emotions observed this event from the back seat of the car. I observed from the passenger seat with my intellect, similar to a recorder, taking in information. The beam was diffused at the top, and the edges of the beam were sharp as a tack, clearly delineated from the blue sky.

To anyone who didn't have my training and practice seeing light and creating visible light in photography, it might appear as simple light. But it wasn't photonic light. It was something else. It started at the level where small aircraft fly, maybe a little higher, and it came down through the windshield to a point as it touched my shoulder. I felt a tangible solid touch.

At that moment of contact with my body, every cell was infused with divine love! Each cell became conscious, just like I feel consciousness in my head right now. Each tiny piece of myself was awakened and responded with love to the love infusing it. I knew myself as trillions of beings. I glanced down at my body as I felt this, and I saw my hand on the steering wheel was glowing a bluish-white from the inside.

I heard a strong, powerful, compassionate, genderless, voice on my right say "Everything will be alright." My soul ascended up the beam. I became the beam. I saw the horizon lower as I arose. As I approached the top I looked up and saw ripples of white and bluish white flowed across the sky.

I became one with the ripples. I was spreading out across the earth. I became one with all the souls on the planet, surrounding the whole earth like the ionosphere. I was one with this field of souls in an embrace of the Earth. I could see the curve of the sphere of the Earth, just like images from space.

Then my focus shifted, and I was one with all the trees on the planet. My focus narrowed even further. I was looking out from a tree in a forest in Colorado. I saw myself in the other trees in the forest. I was looking at my branch hands and knowing it as my own body. I felt the love resonating like a sense of strength and glorious power, with sturdiness, powerfulness, and longevity.

Then my focus shifted and I was one with all the grass on the planet. My focus narrowed some more. I experienced myself as a blade of green grass in Africa. I was also seeing myself in the neighboring blades. I, as grass, was embracing the whole planet. As love, I was reveling in the life, in the detail of expressing myself as grass. It was glorious!

Then my focus shifted again, and I was a rock on a mountain. I felt surprised at being a rock. It was not anything I had ever considered before. I lost my focus from the love, as I was so surprised. I still felt the love, but some part of me was really flabbergasted. "Whoa! I am a rock? Rocks are conscious? Amazing!"

My focused shifted again, the LOVE reestablished primary focus and amplified 100 fold. I WAS THE WHOLE ENTIRE UNIVERSE!! As if all the galaxies were like all the cells in my body - the stars, planets and material, all conscious parts of myself. My arms and my hands were expressed as galaxies, each aware, each an expression of love. My center of consciousness was expanded across the universe. I was IMMENSE and the love that I felt was IMMENSE, IMMENSE, IMMENSE LOVE. So incredible! So amazing! At each level, the intensity of love had increased tenfold, THEN A HUNDRED FOLD!

Then my focus shifted, and I saw the smallest, tiniest particle, in an infinite field of tiny particles that expanded out in all directions in organized rows. I was this field. I was the individual particles. I was the radiance in between them, and as such, I was love and consciousness expressed as the physical. I found I had access to infinite information and potential.

I am going to be as detailed as possible, because as far as I know, this is new information. This is my piece of the puzzle. I had only vaguely been aware of something called "ether" before this, so I had no idea what to call this observation. I called it ether or the unified field in my video, not having any language to even approach describing what I experienced. It took me a little while studying physics to have some idea of what it was that I experienced. I would now say the closest thing to what I experienced that I could find in the physics I learned so far, is the Higgs Field, which may also be dark matter and dark energy. Not to be confused with the Higgs boson which would be much larger than the particles in this field.

The ultimate truth though, is that this field is LOVE, in its most primary physical manifestation. Love which is, by this observation, also the most the primary unit of physicality.

During this part of my experience, I was outside of time and inside of 3 directions of space. I floated through this field of particles in this matrix that extended in every direction. I was conscious and filled with immense love, and I knew myself as this field. Each particle was a perfect white radiant sphere and each was made of love manifested as stuff, as matter. Each particle also emitted or radiated light. This was light that did look more like photonic light to me with some extra properties. The rays of one particle reached and became interwoven in the next particle. None of the particles touched each other. The space between each one was slightly less than the width or diameter of each sphere. They are flexi-fixed in position, and each one has a little wiggle room. I saw a video later where a man uses dry ice to create superconductivity; and it behaved in a similar manner, a little locked at a certain distance. They do not spin from what I perceived, but make tiny little nudges that appeared random to me. Each particle was conscious, and was in fact, LOVE expressed as matter and energy. All the area between the particles was filled with the radiance which was also conscious and love but only as energy, not as matter. The radiance of one particle interwove, intermingled, interacted, interlaced, joined, mended, fused (trying to find the correct word, all of these and more) with the next. It was this interaction that gently yet forcefully held the particles in their respective positions.

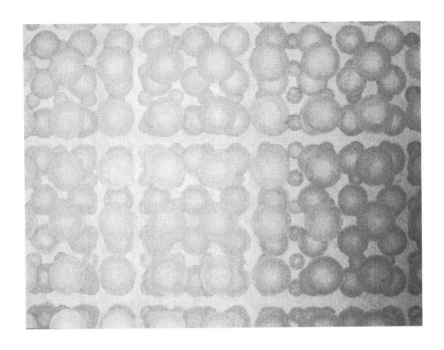

Here I tried to illustrate what I saw, and became. My perspective was gliding through the field of particles at a diagonal and seeing the rows and aisles shift and change as I moved higher and across. As each aisle revealed its path to infinity, I was filled with the breathtaking wonder of its magnificence, complexity and simplicity. I understood that within each particle there was infinite knowledge, infinite consciousness, infinite love and infinite potential. I understood the radiance was filled with infinite information, infinite consciousness and infinite love.

There is a lot more that I have not yet found words to express. Sometimes, when the right question is asked, the answer comes. I also understood this field is the bridge between the physical universe and the non physical.

Now after years of processing my experience, I believe it is this field that makes instantaneous knowing across great distances, for example like from Dhaka, Bangladesh to Irvine, California, USA, possible.

Then my focus shifted once more, and I went into what I call the Vast or Vast Void. By appearance, the Vast Void is nothing - black. But it is more accurately EVERYTHING, BEFORE IT BECOMES SOMETHING. "Un-time" is indistinguishable from ALL TIME. "Un-space" is incredibly dense with what is yet to be space. I found myself immersed and infused in a thousand-fold more love, infinitely more love, indescribable love. Whereas the love of the beam was describable as the love of a parent for their infant child, this love in the Vast far exceeded that love. (If I allow myself to come close to that level of love as I remember my experience of the Vast, I just lose all control and have to sob. It's almost unbearable to go there emotionally, like my body can't deal with even a fraction of that much love, even now writing this.)

As I transitioned the field to the next experience, I passed through something like an event horizon, where I "GOT" all the knowledge, all information and became all knowing, omniscient. From within the field of particles just before this, I had ACCESS to all knowledge. In the Vast Void, now I AM all knowledge and information and I know everything. No need to ask and get answers. I was, in concept, VAST! That is my personal way to relate this sense, using a spatial framework. I say "in concept" because I was outside of time and space and even concept, but I want to try to convey some sense of what it was like.

When I felt the souls, the trees, the grass, the rocks, the universe, and the particles, I was inside of space but outside of time. But the Vast Void was outside of time and space. The whole universe which had an instant ago been so tangible and real, seemed now a mere fleeting thought by comparison to this ultra, hyper, super, mega reality.

This experience either looked black, or there was just no visual data to translate as a visual perception. What was there, was immense information and energy that was as yet un-manifest. Unexpressed potential. Pure energy prior to actualization. Most of this data has no reference point in this physical reality. I, as omniscient, was source to the universe, but also source to some other indescribable un-reference-able creation. Never in this experience was there love without consciousness or consciousness without love. The level of both is so incredibly intense and ecstatic. Every word falls short at reaching the depths. There is no vocabulary to express the grandeur and magnificence of the experience. So incredible! So amazing! I want to just open my heart and transmit this emotion in a download to every soul on the planet. I want to pour it out and unload this love directly to your heart. It is not me, Mary, that is the "I" that I speak of here. It is the One Self that we all are. The same self is in you. Present at your own level of awakening, to knowing the divine self that you are. You are the "I" in this. There is no difference between the "I" that each one of us refers to. I AM you and you are me. This is not an experience of the individuated small me only. This is your potential or may already be your actual experience.

I can understand why some religions refer to this part as "The Void" and use negative terms like "nothing" to talk about it. Superficially it appears like nothing. It is true that it is "no thing." It is not material; it is intangible. It is pure energy before it is anything. By pure, I mean lowest possible entropy, perhaps even negative entropy. There is no time because it is outside of timespace/spacetime. Even though I like the term Vast there is no information of space in this experience. Maybe the word energy is false in the same way space and time words are false because it is Love and Consciousness before it is even converted to energy. Energy before it is energy, potential energy. Time is a part of the physical construct that allows experience to be narrowly focused.

The word experience fails too, because it is even more primary than that. Awareness or being or existence are better words to express that it is deep and core. Love and Consciousness are the best words if they have to stand alone, but stripped of all the cultural, and romantic, religious and scientific connotations. However, understand that where we always separate these two concepts, they are somehow merged as one ultra-real, ultra-pure being-ness. The feeling that went along with having all the knowledge, being all of the knowledge, was a complete fullness, a really delightfully, wonderfully slaked feeling. In my family, we have this saying when we finish a meal. We ask "Are you sufficiently suffonsified?" and the answer is "Yes, I am sufficiently suffonsified, and any more would be rude to my capacity." So having all the knowledge, information, wisdom, savvy, computability, intellect - every different format of knowledge - I felt suffonsified to the max. I understood, and was able to retain this truth, so that I may share that the physical universe is created so that the "Divine Oneself" can EXPERIENCE "Self" as "Other". From the Divine Oneself's perspective, because experience as other is the primary purpose of the physical universe, any experience as "other" is highly valuable.

Track 2

I have to backtrack in telling the story because what I shared so far was only one part of this simultaneous experience. As I mentioned previously, I heard a voice on my right say, "EVERTHING WILL BE ALRIGHT." It was external to my ear and clearly audible. It did not have gender, but it did have power and meaning and depth and presence and love.

Then I was suddenly back fully in my body. The part that was in the passenger seat and the part that was in the back seat rejoined my physical body too. My level of consciousness was also back to relatively normal (for me anyway).

I said out loud to myself, "That just happened" (matter-of-fact tone). I felt awed! Then with all the emotion of a totally impressed teenager I said out loud "COOOOOOL!!! That was so totally cooooool!"

And then I realized the pain was completely gone, as if it had never been.

Track 3

At the same time, I felt a download of information go into the back left side of my brain. I have yet to unpack it, but I know it is there, and I will have access when the time is right.

Track 4

In the instant the white beam was reaching down and touching my shoulder, there was also a radiant golden light surrounding the Barnes and Noble sign. The sign was not turned on yet. So the radiant golden halo of illumination surrounding the sign was not from the sign itself. I then understood that God wanted me to go to the bookstore.

I had one second to decide and act, and I quickly turned the wheel and took the exit to go to the shopping center.

One of the immediate thoughts that crossed my mind was, "'Wow, if God is that powerful and that incredible, what a total rip off that almost no one gets to experience God! And why ever not, when it felt like the most natural thing that I ever experienced?" I wished I could upload this love to the world. I envisioned a beam of golden light similar to a sky spotlight coming out of my heart and torso as a way of being able to share this feeling directly with others.

I then asked in my heart, "Who was that?" I heard in my mind the reply, "God of Abraham." This God of Abraham was very different from what I had learned in my religion, or even what I read in the Bible. The words "God of Abraham" repeated in my head for months afterward.

Any pain that I had been feeling from my earlier heartache was gone, as if it have never happened in the first place. This experience blew out any doubt I had remaining of God's existence. It also dissolved all the preconceived ideas I had learned from my 12 years of Catholic school, and all the other reading and research I had done about who and what God is.

I am not saying necessarily that anyone is wrong, but that we are really challenged when it comes to expressing the ineffable. It used to piss me off to hear people get to "ineffable" in their description and vowed that if it ever happened to me I would not say ineffable because it is a copout.

This is just the uncomfortable truth. We won't be able to get there until we get there. The good news is that we don't have to die to get there.

13 ∞ Now What?

In the bookstore, I felt completely separated from the experience, so I meandered around bewildered. I wondered, "Now What?" There were so many books, and I felt really overwhelmed and unguided. I wandered aimlessly hoping I would get a vibe or a pull in a direction. Among the many books, there was one book that caught my eye, but when I looked at the description, it was about math. As someone who could not calculate the tip on a restaurant bill, I thought, "No way, and besides it was not on sale, and God knows I am cheap and don't pay full price for books." I took a moment to appreciate that even after all that had just happened, I was still arguing with God.

I picked out another book instead and went home. The math book, however, would not get out of my head and I kept seeing the cover of the book flashing in my mind's eye like an annoying woodpecker. I called in sick that Friday and went back to the bookstore and bought the book, paying full price, and my budget never even noticed the hit.

The book was "The Mystery of the Aleph" by Amir D. Aczel, and it was about math, as well as the biography of Georg Cantor. But this was not just regular math. It was abstract math, and I dove right in and finished the book in 12 hours. Miraculously, I understood it too. It was about set theory, and as I read more and more it became apparent to me that this was a mathematical way to express what I had just experienced.

If you take an infinite set of numbers like one to infinity, you can then take a subset of those numbers (like all of the odd numbers) that is also infinite, and then the subset is equal to the set. It is a true paradox. Subset = Set. $\infty = \infty$ It shouldn't be true, but it is true. That truth in itself expresses how we ourselves are infinite. The Vast Void is the original, infinite, source set, and everything else is a subset. There is infinite potential in every cell, in every molecule, in every atom and in every part of the Higgs field. Infinite Love and infinite Consciousness exist in every subset. Everything in existence is a subset of the "Whole Divine Set." The universe is a subset of "The Vast." "The Everything" does not come out of "Nothing," aka the Void. "The Everything" comes out of the "Source Set" which, although it may appear like nothing or something "other," is in fact SELF, the ultimate One-Self which we all are. When you drill down into the core and find the source, you find Love as Self. Infinite Love, Infinite Self.

There are an endless number of subsets of the infinite set. Each infinite subset is equal to the original set. Love and consciousness are in ultimate reality, infinite. Opening my being to this infinite consciousness is how I perceived the tiniest particle matrix, containing infinity. In the space between the particles there is infinity. In atoms there is infinity. In cells there is infinity. Not just infinity, but infinite love and infinite consciousness. There is infinite potential in each of these forms of physicality. There appear to be limits, but those limits are only illusions.

Limits can be useful subsets. The assumption of a finite set is usually reasonable, for example the separation between one person and the next. It is rational to conclude each person is separate. But if you think about it for a minute, you can understand that where one person stops and the next person starts is not always clearly delineated. Is your smell a part of you? What if I breath it in, does it become a part of me? Since every subset is part of the set, and the set is infinite, consider the limits may be abstract, derived, or made up.

In photons, its infinite. In electrons, its infinite. In every type, angle, dimension - every way you look at it - whether you put it all together or break it all apart, there are infinitudes in each subset of physical reality, just like there are infinities in the numbers. So the entire physical universe is an infinity, but also within the cell there is an infinity. Within the molecule there is an infinity. Within the Higgs field there is an infinity. But it's not just infinity, it is endless consciousness, everlasting love and unlimited potential. That's the information that I was given.

Within each of us is this amazing infinite love and consciousness, at the core of our being, through and through, up and down, in and out, left and right - Love and Consciousness. We have access to that information, that being, that place, that understanding, that Divine Love, that incredible power. And we have it through the experience of self. Although we can find Divinity in everyone and everything, we don't need to look outside of ourselves. We can find that Divinity within ourselves. We are magnificent and LOVED! You are loved and lovable! You are Divine!

14 ∞ Oneself

I had a really hard time processing that information for my own individuated self. In fact, I still struggle with that. It's not the easiest thing to assimilate, and the thing that challenged me the most was accepting and believing that about others. After my experience, I was fully and completely healed of the hurt that my fiancé caused me. But there were other hurts from my childhood that were not healed. I was flabbergasted that I could experience God and still feel pain in any way, but there it was. So I decided I was going to set childhood pain aside for my next lifetime. It took me years and years to get around to processing that pain and finally heal it.

That healing came by way of a Reiki attunement. I went to classes to learn Reiki energy healing, and the night before my second Reiki attunement class, I had a dream that healed me from my childhood pain. That dream helped me to understand that even the most evil people are made of love. Even the most evil people are children of God from God's perspective. Maybe not from our perspective, and that's fine. We don't have to be at the level of God consciousness every minute of every day. We have the potential to flow in and out of various levels of consciousness depending on the situation.

I was in that Divine level of consciousness for those moments during my experience and I have been able to get back there on occasion. But it is not an every-minute-of-every-day thing for me. When it happens, it's really awesome, but it's not all the time. It's OK that it's not. It's normal that sometimes you get angry and frustrated and feel pain and whatever else is happening. It's all OK; everything is alright. It's playing out perfectly. Of course when you are in that very deep pain, it doesn't feel OK for you in that moment, but it's perfect in the bigger scheme of things. There is a higher purpose for everything. Everything has meaning. Every experience to the most fleeting thought is valuable because it is important to God - our GODSELF.

The concept of God from my childhood upbringing is that God is omniscient, omnipresent and omnipotent, and that's true. But I think the experience of the Vast Void more closely correlates with the idea of the Holy Spirit. The idea of the Holy Spirit is not well understood by pretty much anybody. What is the Holy Spirit? Some flame on your head? That's not it. The Holy Spirit is the ONE-SOUL that we all are. Some people want to separate themselves, their own identity, from the Divine Self and that's fine. You can hold yourself separate so that you can understand it. The ultimate truth is that we are not separate from the Divine Self. We are the Divine Self! The Divine Self and we are one and the same.

Imagine we individuated selves are the villi, which are the absorption filaments in our small intestine of God, (gross analogy, I know). We are here to absorb physicality and experience it for the Divine. We are the sensory organs for God. God is expressing through US. Collectively we are our Godself. Individually we are also expressing our Godself yet mostly unaware that we are doing so. We all have the potential to access the Godself, Oneself, or Holy Spirit that is ever-present within us.

I flow in and out of the oneness and being separate. Consider viewing earth from the space station, seeing a hurricane pattern one can appreciate its beauty. From really high up, events are more abstract and things present as flat. Processes are appreciated from a different experiential and emotional perspective. From an expanded vantage point, the ebb and flow of nature can be respected and treasured.

When you get down here to the surface level, there is a lot of wind activity, bumpiness and chaos. For most of us, from an individuated consciousness perspective, down here on planet earth, there is duality, good, bad, benevolent and malevolent. However, from the Divine GodSelf unity consciousness perspective, everything is important. Everything is valuable, loved, and appreciated.

Out of unity consciousness, individuation forms. As soon as there is individuation, there is separation. As soon as there is separation there is "other" and personality, and ego, and free will, and the potential for differing wills and drama.

15 ∞ What About...?

Always in the back of my mind was the idea that an enlightenment experience has to be repeated, and it has to be able to be shared or corroborated for it to be credible evidence.

After a while, when I hadn't yet had another experience, and I was getting kind of intense about it, I went to bed and I prayed really hard. With clear intention that something would happen, I decided I am going back to the love of the Vast Void. To home.

I also had a burning question, "What about angels and demons and all the other beings from heaven and hell that other people reported? Is that all true or not?" Since what I had experienced up to this point seemed to be the ultimate in the Divine

Consciousness, I wondered, "Were all those other people who have been reporting these other experiences delusional or lying? What's the deal, God?"

It happened during sleep, and after review, it was clearly an out-of-body-experience (OBE) - actually a series of out-of-body-experiences. I went to bed, and went right to sleep. I woke up from this extraordinary experience at 3:33. I went back into the same "dream" sequence and woke up again at 4:44, and again at 5:55 and then at 7:07.

The initial segment began at what I will refer to as "level 3." So it seems I skipped levels one and two and jumped ahead. It was the "classical heaven" - a breathtakingly beautiful environment. Although I did see specific environments in all of these experiences, I also inherently knew that what I was experiencing was not all there is to experience.

As I fall asleep, I find myself in a beautiful setting. There is a crystal palace, another regular palace or castle, and beautiful manicured gardens, trees and pastures. It is populated, but not over-populated. There is a feeling of bliss, peace, and Divine

Love. There are happy people, joyful pastel colors, and a vibrancy of life force, intelligence and consciousness. Everything and everyone is happy. It's like a wonderful party. It's comfortable.

On this level beings are mostly human as far as I can see. The souls are individuated and don't necessarily know everything. At level 3 it feels very visual, very spatial and tangible. There is nothing negative at all; it's just heavenly, literally. The heaven that people talk about, classical heaven, is level 3.

The next segment of experience in which I find myself I'll refer to as "level 4." There is also a palace on level 4. There is infinite food here (yeah, that's what I'm talking about!). I am personally really pleased in this area. There is an area full of friends and love. People know each other more fully. Everyone seems to be my very best friend or family and loves me deeply. Every one of them is in a state of joy and bliss to see me. The love flows in and floods my perception. On level 4, there is a school. There is access to more information than level 3. On this level an spirit can ask questions and get answers. At level 4 there is guidance, and there are guides helping you. Actually, there are guides everywhere, but level 4 has more to do with being of service, learning and the exchange of information and ideas, whereas on level 3 there is such a sense of peace and joy.

Level 4 has more motion and purposeful action. I visit the palace and walk along a marble patio with massive columns. At the end of the patio there is a treasure chest. I am thrilled that I am abundant. I immediately reach my hands in and scoop up a bunch of rubies, emeralds, crystals and other gems and put them into the lifted front hem of my T-shirt so that I can take them back with me. My guide laughs. I sense him shaking his head, as if to say, "You can try. Go ahead. Take some." I feel my guide by my side, but just out of sight during the whole journey.

When I woke up at 4:44, I checked my shirt and there was nothing there, and I thought, "Oh man, I thought I was gonna be rich!"

The Journey continues from where it left off, during the next segment of the evening. I go up from level 4. Between level 4 and 5 there is a membrane or some kind of boundary or density that filters or prevents some souls from ascending higher. Level 5 is where you reach the level of omniscience, having all the information available to you. On this level you no longer need to ask questions, but you still need to direct your focus to what you want to think about. Level 5 has group souls.

I continue to Level 6. Here and above is where the Divine heavenly beings reside - angels, guides, and beings similar to the Egyptian, Hindu, Greek and Roman Gods. I don't experience any specific demigods there, but it is the sense I get of the residents at this level.

When someone dies, they can enter at any level depending on their individual consciousness. They may be able to ascend or descend to other levels.

Later I learned that level 6 is where councils are maintained. These advanced beings originate or resonate at an even higher frequency, so they can go to any and all levels. However, not everyone can get to the elevated levels. During this segment of my heavenly journey, I go all the way up to the supreme heavenly realm before the Vast Void.

At the uppermost realm before the Vast is "incorporation of individuation." I understand that it is at this highest level that individuation starts to happen - like the creation of archangels - but somewhat more nebulous than that. It is consciousness just slightly separated. I perceive these individuations as supernatural beings of some kind. They seem to be entities of the highest frequency. They are individuated, but still really connected to unity consciousness and to each other. There is also an omnipresent aspect to these beings.

At the highest level, the slightly individuated beings may not even have what we would call an identity, and nothing like a name. It might be something like a force or a law. It's very hard to put these ideas into words.

16 ∞ Return to the Vast Void

I go into the Vast Void and this time I recognize it because I have been there before. The level of love and consciousness is immense but there is no visual information, so it looks like emptiness or black. There is no "formation." At the same time, there is a knowing of all information at once. Supreme intelligence that not only knows all the information but can also think all the knowledge at once. I am ecstatic with the feeling I have returned home, in this loving beingness of darkness.

All of a sudden a structured light in a geodesic orb or sphere appears before me. It is an intelligent, loving being. It knows me and loves me. Shards of crisp light pierce the darkness. It has sections of what look to me like emptiness. In the emptiness there are little lights moving, dancing, going in jigs, in circles and half circles. Each section is a triangle, pentagon or octagon, and in between the sections are bands of light. The light is there; then there is nothing; then these floating tiny lights appear. The lines of luminosity that separate the shapes are pulsing. The whole thing gets bigger and smaller. Pulsing. A motion similar to expanding and contracting - or breathing. I am amazed! At this level, there is SO MUCH LOVE. I bask in the love, in deep saturated awe.

And then I wake up again. Awake enough to write down the highlights of my experience in my notebook before going right back to sleep and into the experience again.

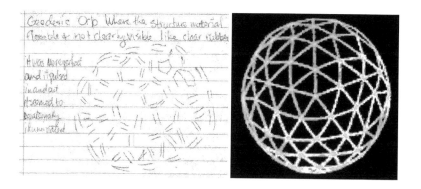

17 ∞ Pause Before the Gate of Hell

Remember this is not an architectural draft. It is just my personal way of organizing the information so that I can hold onto it, understand it and talk about it. All the words are my best approximation of the concepts.

Even though I declare in what seems like absolute and certain terms - which is the feeling I have with this information - I allow that I did not experience everything there is to experience in heaven and on earth. I am as certain that I did not experience everything as I feel certain about what I did experience. So do I feel certain about what I know? Yes. Am I certain? Yes. But only to the extent that certainty is possible for one individuation that does not fully sustain unity consciousness.

I feel it is important before these next sections to acknowledge that our ability to respond begins when we have awareness of our ability to respond and not before. Understanding that we create our own suffering is not the same as being responsible for it. But at the moment we become aware of our own part in the creation process, that moment is when we become able to respond in the present. So there is no need to beat ourselves up over the past transgressions, but today with that knowledge we can learn from them and inform our ability to respond and consciously create better.

18 ∞ Neither Here Nor There

So you think when you get to the top of heaven you'll be done.

I find myself in another void, but this void is empty. Potentially scary. This void is more like nothing. Some areas appear grey or blue. It feels like a I am just waiting, like in a weigh station. I don't have much information of place, just barely place, a spacious non-space, lacking any of the information of the vast void. No thoughts. More like forgetfulness, than a peaceful thoughtlessness. There is nobody here. As I hang out, I begin to feel peaceful and pleasant and some thoughts begin to form. For reference, I'll call this level 1, although I could not say for sure where in the frequency continuum it belongs.

Then I find myself in a place that looks like a copy of earth, except it is still pretty much empty.

I find myself in a home, in someone's living room, where there is a metaphysical class being held. The class is teaching how to enter a person's body. When it is my turn, I enter this person. I stand them up, and I flail their arms about to show that I can. Part of me has the thought that other people seeing this person moving their arms about will still not know that it is a second person inhabiting the body. But apparently the teacher and those in the class, and of course the person who's body I have entered, all know what is happening. When I exit the body, the energy and the time have altered drastically. I expect rejoicing, but I find myself in a dark empty room. Apparently many hours or days have passed. The others are gone. I am alone. I feel a deep loneliness that touches my soul beyond words, a deep emptiness, a lost and forgotten feeling, like being in an emotional abyss, although the room generally looks the same.

I know something is very much "not right." I look at the clock which says 25:25, confirming something is not right. I pray "God please take me to the right time and place, now." I open my eyes and the clock still reads 25:25. How can that not have worked? Praying always worked before. So I pray even more intensely, feeling my intention clearly in my mind.

Still 25:25. I pray again more fervently, feeling my passion reach down to my heart. I slowly open my eyes. The clock still glares mockingly 25:25.

I am confused, frustrated and starting to feel out of my depth! Maybe I am really stuck in some non-physical dimension! I pray once more, this time with every ounce of intensity I can muster, feeling it reach my whole being from head to groin, finally accessing my whole will, which until this experience I have never accessed before. I open my eyes. I am in my room. The clock reads 7:07.

I was so relieved! Every detail of that journey is still emblazoned in my memory.

19 ∞ I'm Going Back In....

I still had lots of unanswered questions. What about the devils and demons? And was empty earth-like experience or waiting place hell?

Not long after that night, I have another dream state out-of-body-experience (OBE).

I find myself in a crowded location with unimaginably hideous beings. I am frightened and horrified! After only milliseconds, I am back in my body.

Even though it was wholly terrifying, I felt some level of success at having gone there. It was in heaven "level 2" or hell. Hell, I now understand is just a part of HEaven level II = HEII. I eventually learn it is a realm that has a lot of

VARIETY in the way that it appears and the way that it can be experienced.

I decided I wanted to know more about hell, and more about where all these other beings are coming from. I still felt intense curiosity and had these questions that I really wanted answered. So I tried it again a few days later. I set the intention to go back in and to feel the fear and just sustain it and tough it out as long as possible. I never really questioned if it was possible, or wise, or had any other thoughts of limitations. It was just something I wanted to know, and I felt OK to ask anything. I had the intention that I would and could find out what I wanted to know. I was not going to accept that there is any mystery I can't uncover. I was also clear in my intention that I was seeking and getting true answers and not merely lucid dreaming.

Once in the OBE, I become aware of being conscious. I find I am in a mass of beings - all these different creatures in a crowded place. No, not creatures; it is too demeaning and de-humanizing of a word. It puts too much separation between us. I can only say the beings are hideous because there is some defense mechanism that prevents me from retaining the detail of their appearance. Again I am immersed to the depths of my soul in terror, yet somehow I manage to stand my ground and just be there. I am trying to beat down my terror, or let it flow like standing in a torrent of a river. I just barely manage to stay calm, when I become aware of this massive dragon next to me. He is very intimidating. I am frightened, yet I am determined to stand my ground. I decide I am just going to be here and experience whatever there is to experience, with waves of terror going through me.

The dragon comes close to me. He has the appearance of a medieval dragon with horns, and bumps, and texture to the hide. He is a deep eggplant color, with a gloss that picks up the highlights of the available light. I say "he" because that is the sense I have. The environment is very dark though, and so populated, and with such activity, it is difficult to focus on any one element.

Suddenly there is peace. I feel a bubble of love and protection envelop me like a warm loving hug. I am able to sense this love is emanating off of this magnificent Dragon. His head is three times bigger than me. He drops his head down to my level, his eye slit directly in front of me, and says telepathically, "See with your heart." I bring my focus down from where my head would be, to where my heart would be, and I open up my heart. It's like a feeling that I kind of expand, putting my focus down to where my emotions are. With this expansion of focus, I can experience this horrifying environment without fear. Absolutely NO FEAR! It is *really* empowering to be here and to release my terror. Because I was just feeling overwhelming terror! Then an instant later, no, I'm good. I'm good. I'm fine. It's okaaay! I feel indomitable! I also know in my heart that everyone is sourced from the vast infinite Divine Love - that everything and everyone is created from love, of love, even this place and these beings.

"OK, I'm gonna look." I begin to look around. I feel better than okay now. This environment is really crowded with so many scary-looking beings. I can't even tell how many. I reach out with my heart and feel the area, just as the Dragon suggested. I receive data, sort of like a sonar bounce of the area. I instantly perceive lots of information which was previously unavailable. In this moment, I understand all the entities there are playing out their particular drama. This is just the thing their soul needs for their own personal spiritual evolution. I understand that each scenario is working out elements specific to those players.

As I stand here, in the bubble of loving protection, in this brief instant of losing my fear, the crowd parts and a path opens up. It extends across the area, a space of about 30 feet. There are a few steps up to a raised platform with a massive throne.

Seated on the uncomfortably hard-looking throne of marble is this magnificent horned creation. This being has a muscular body-builder chest. His face is mostly human, but really edgy and bull-like. His jaw line is really chiseled. He has a really powerful nose, and his eyes are amber. His is a deep reddish mahogany. What really strikes me are the horns coming out of his head near where the hairline is! The horns extend up from his forehead in opposite gentle spirals. They are covered in a satiny hide and not bone. They are also that same dark mahogany color as his face with a highlight glancing off their satin sheen.

If I was still terrified, I would have just completely lost it! But I am not in terror. I am feeling safe and secure within the Dragon's protection field. Seeing this horned being with my heart allows me to perceive more information! This being is not a terrorizor. I can see that he is a servant and is performing a service. He provides order. My eyes connect with his and I "get" that he is a STEWARD for this place and his service is in holding the energy at this particular frequency so that all of these stories have a place to unfold as these souls need.

This magnificent being looks out with deep compassion. His expression speaks volumes; not at all seeking sympathy, but conveying an understanding that he has been getting a bad rap, and that he has lovingly accepted this honor and most challenging responsibility. I feel his own - not exactly suffering - but endurance, or enduring devotion, to the terribly difficult task bestowed upon him. He is doing exactly what needs to be done, holding the energetic space, and he will continue this service eternally, or until all the dramas are resolved, whichever happens first.

I look with my heart. I can see that there are a lot of good beings, "Benevolent Uglies." It takes a powerfully loving soul to be in this place offering assistance and solace to those who suffer. Just because something is ugly doesn't mean that it is bad. Even for me when I am looking with my heart they are sooo hideous.

Without the experience of the unconditional love of the Vast, and the protection of the Dragon, I would not able to endure this environment very long. The level of pain the beings are experiencing is inconceivable. Malevolent demons also play a part in these tragic events. Seeing with my heart makes it possible for me to discern between good and evil. I comprehend that the whole process of evil and the beings experiencing a suffering role is not because of a punishment by the Divine Oneself, or a judgment of God for not meeting certain conditions. The only judgment or punishment is self-assigned by the individuated level of consciousness.

Some beings are doing the terrorizing and it is horrible, worse than can be imagined or spoken of. However, from the highest level of understanding, I recognize both roles of perpetrator and victim have significance to themselves, each other and to the Divine Oneself. I am not given any of the details of why any particular being has any particular experience, just that somehow it has value to them in the grand scheme of things.

I try to communicate with one of the victims, but they do not respond to my attempts. I offer assistance again. I say, "This experience is not the way it has to be. " This time I do have some success in helping the soul to lift up out of the depths and awaken enough to realize they can ask for help.

20 ∞ Suffering: Good and Evil

I realize when we are operating in and from a lower state of consciousness, we can be - and are - hurt. We can be - and are - in pain, and suffer mental and physical anguish. One path to change our state, is to become aware that there is another way; then muster the courage and humility to admit we could use some help, and ask for it.

That alone may raise our vibration somewhat. Further evolution comes from acting from an emotional and mental state of compassion and love. We may be able to attune to love with the assistance of others. In the OBE, that's what the Dragon does for me.

By understanding good and evil as roles we are playing, it does not imply there is a justification for evil. Not all sources of evil may be reached with love, because of free will. Some malevolent malefactors can lie convincingly. There are also entities that can change the way they look. We should be aware of the dangers.

I learned by tuning into my heart and soul in level 2, that at some point there is an aspect of our own participation in the creation of the drama. This drama unfolds through various manifestations of ego, such as stubbornness, resistance, fear, hatred, or anger. There could be many reasons, including a desire of our higher self to experience separateness or chaos. We may just be expressing our free will.

Once I knew I made the choices for my story, I questioned it. "I chose THIS? Are you kidding me?" But it is the way it is. "I locked myself out from my memory? Why did I do this?" It doesn't make sense at this level of information, but it makes sense at the higher level of information. It makes perfect sense. We feel and see suffering from such a different perspective, when we attune to our higher selves. It gives us a different value set, so that we make different decisions.

When I found myself in heaven level 2, this Hell-like consciousness where people are free to process baggage, I learned if at any moment I wanted to change my state, I could. I simply prayed "God please help me!!!" As I discovered, I have to really mean it, to the very deepest depths of my soul. In this frequency of creation, my thoughts and prayers are created instantly. My authentic intentions are revealed in the non-physical reality.

Raising my vibration in the density of physical reality may be more challenging but is still possible, especially when I can stay attuned to the Divine Oneself.

The attunement piece of this process is huge! I realize that that is what reading the spiritual books did for me. It attuned me. Eating healthy food also helped to calibrate me. It makes me realize I still have room for improvement. I can now consciously include more high frequency things like exercise, nature, the ocean, the stars, the sun, cats and babies.

The truth is, God Loves all beings and all of creation. All is created by love, from love, for love and if you consider that the Divine Oneself even loves these malevolent beings, then you can surely understand that God dearly loves you.

21 ∞ Heaven's Heavens

I came to organize these experiences into three categories of reality.

Physical reality: That is where we are presently. We perceive it physically with the five primary senses. It is the most common definition of reality. For some, physical reality includes some overlap of information from other people and not only our own perception.

Higher reality: That is where I visited these environments of soul evolution. In higher reality, as soon as individuation happens, there is some sense of separation. Separation is not real, in that it is instantly not the whole story! As reality goes, higher reality has more information than physical reality, like having more lines of code.

Ultimate reality: This is the Vast Void beyond heaven, the Divine Oneself, the unity, the love consciousness, and energy, pure and unified. This is the most true, based on all I have experienced! Everything else is true, but not the whole truth. Ultimate reality has all the information, accessible all at once, with no separation.

I am going to focus here on higher reality because this is where most of the confusion comes in. The various environments at different stages of spiritual evolution that I describe, are divided into arbitrary divisions just so I can process the information.

The extra data of higher reality includes not only the emotional content of others, but also the clear access to thoughts relationships and story. The information included in higher reality can be delivered through similar perception channels, just like the 5 senses, even though at some frequencies there is no actual body. For example, one can know the consciousness of others. One can know the thoughts, emotions and identity of others, all without being told or receiving that information through specific senses. At times the information does come through what seems like a sense process.

22 ∞ Super States

It is reasonable that people hearing about these types of experiences for the first time might question their validity. So I put some thought into analyzing why it is so immediately clear to me that these experiences are real, as opposed to a dream. Even with thorough research of the hundreds of anecdotal experiences reported around the world, it's still reasonable to be skeptical. Empaths, psychics and mediums have their own validation from direct access to information from other people, places, times and things. For those who haven't had personal validations, or aren't sure, let's examine the different experiential states from imagination, memory and dreams to visions, visitations, prophecies, past lives, and out-of-body experiences. I know there are a lot of people who have sincere questions about this.

How do I tell the difference between various experiential states? I carefully study the information available from my experiences, and from the many people I speak to who have had near death and other transformational experiences.

We can't take a camera or recording device to document these journeys, so our own power of observation is the only tool we have with us in the non-physical realms.

I can only analyze the information by using all of my sensory and extrasensory perceptions to differentiate one state from another state. In order to compare, I need to closely look at what I can distinguish of physical reality. As I mentioned in chapter two, most people have access to the data from only their own five senses. They may additionally experience memories, dreams and imagination. Some people, like me, may also perceive emotions, thoughts and other information using more than five senses.

Visitations, out-of-body experiences, past lives, and prophecy are glimpses into higher reality, but since they are filtered through our physical body, we may not get all the data. When these experiences have heightened emotion, detailed sense acuity and increased memory retention, then that is a good indication that they are accessing information from higher reality. I can discern different experiential states by the level and intensity of this sensory data.

Imagination

When I am using my imagination there is always information that is missing. It's important to note, because no matter how much detail I put into my visualizations, I cannot successfully recreate the level of detail of physical reality or higher reality. Imagination, even if you are imagining something bad is going to happen, is a mental choice. A vision, on the other hand, is a surprise. It feels very clearly not self-generated.

Dreams

When you have a dream, even though you can have a dream that is ultra vivid, there is often missing data - rules that are broken. There's always something that tips you off and clues you in that this is a dream, and not a memory.

Some dreams you can track to events of the day, your physical life, something in your past, or even a movie you have just seen. We do have regular dreams where we work out our stuff and process emotions. We also have wish fulfillment dreams.

There are several experiential states that may seem like dreams or may actually use a dream as a vehicle. Visitations, premonitions and OBE's can all be revealed in a dream state.

23 ∞ Visitation

A visitation is either something or someone from a higher reality coming into your dream, meditation or waking state. If a visitation comes in a dream, it is an infusion of higher reality into a lower state. Many people report being able to remember this kind of experience with hyper clarity. If a spirit arrives in the physical, there is an overlap of the physical and higher reality. Different types of visitations include dream visits, mediumship, channeling, haunting, poltergeists and spiritual embodiment. Visitors may be deceased relatives, pets, angels, guides, God or anything.

Code Word: Umbrella

I went to see the famous medium John Edward when he was in San Diego. My mom and my siblings saw him when he was in Ohio. That prompted a conversation with my Mom before she passed, where she said, that if she could get a message through, she would come through with the umbrella story. Specifically, she wanted it to be something unlikely, so that it would be convincing.

Sometime after my mom passed, my friend invited me to go a Joanne Gerber mediumship demonstration. My friend and I were both lucky that Joanne brought through many spirits for us including my mom. Among many other verifiable details, she said " Umbrella! There is a thing about an umbrella." That was one more solid piece of evidence for me that consciousness exists beyond the physical.

The Umbrella Story: One day my mom went to the drugstore, and it started to rain. She had forgotten her umbrella, and when she arrived there, a stranger in the parking lot walked her to the store under his umbrella. When she finished her shopping, there was an umbrella in the lost and found for her. She knew then that she would never have to worry about having an umbrella; one would always be provided for her. And so it was the case, she reported, as she shared this story some 40 years after it happened.

24 ∞ Out-of-body Experiences

Unlike the glimpses you get from within the body, like a vision or a visitation, an out-of-body experience (OBE) may give you access to the full data set, depending on how deep into higher reality you go. You are literally out of your body. You may or may not be able to see your body, but you are out, and you know you are out. You can stay anchored to time and space, or you can transcend time and space, as you choose. Your direction and experience can be guided by your clear intention or divinely directed. An OBE where you go to higher dimensions slips off the consciousness buffering filter of the body. Thought becomes crystal clear and fast. All senses become amplified. You know yourself as more than a physical being. You recognize your body is not who you really are.

Angels Talk

In an out-of-body experience of note, I heard the Angels! At the beginning of this OBE I am blissfully flying around. Then I meet up with a man who seems as tall as a basketball player, but I have the feeling it is my friend Dr. Al Taylor (who happens to have written a book about astral travel, *Soul Traveler: A Guide to Out-of-Body Experiences and the Wonders Beyond*. I feel a sense of familiarity, but he is not that tall. Good to know we can appear any way we would like to in the astral plane. He says "Oh my gosh! I can't believe you are here!" As he guides me, we continue together flying around the general Los Angeles area.

He takes me to a place where there is a swimming pool. We are diving in and out of the water to feel what it feels like to be astral in the water. It feels like I can still breathe under the water. It is really FUN!

We fly to this mall in Hollywood. I can see the Hollywood sign, and there is an escalator. I am going up the escalator, and at the next level up, the floors are very fantastically luxurious, like marble. Then there is another level of escalators going up.

I start to go up, and my guide says, "Oh you're not supposed to go up there." I say, "Why not? I want to see what's up there." I ride up the second level of escalators, and instead of taking me to another level of the mall, it starts to take me up to heaven. My guide doesn't come with me on the second level of escalators.

At the top of the escalator it emerges into a nebulous non-physical area that is all white. I see these very tall beings of light. I can also hear what sounds to me like soprano vocalizations. My lovely blissful feeling gets even better as I listen. I think, "Oh my gosh, that is so beautiful! Such a beautiful sound!" Then I try to do it myself. I try to mimic the sounds because I want to see what that is like. So I start vocalizing and I begin doing my version of whatever I think they are doing. Then a light being comes over to me, and sends me the telepathic message, "We are not singing. We are talking to each other." It feels to me as if the light being is lovingly amused by my silliness. "What!? You are talking to each other!?" I exclaim. Confused, I pause and listen, but I can't get past how beautiful it sounds. It doesn't make sense to me at all as language. I am only able to understand the telepathic message.

I have since been trying to find something similar in any kind of earthly music and the closest thing is Steven Halpern's piece "Gift of the Angels," a very high soprano in some other language or in no language at all. Years later, when I visited Hollywood & Highland Center in Hollywood, I recognized it as the same place as this OBE.

Verifiable OBE

Once you can get out of your body, you can go pretty much anywhere or any-when. Some experiences I can't verify. So other than the value of the experience itself - for my own spiritual evolution and the inherent joy they brought me, as they were very ecstatically fun - they did not provide more than anecdotal evidence.

Another time, I specifically set the intention to experience something that could be verified. As soon as I realized I was out of my body, I first had to dampen my elation, because I knew it could send me back in. Then I thought, "Take me to my mother." I was immediately rushing across the country from California to Ohio, seeing plots of farmland shooting by below! I was being pulled from my torso, and I was positioned vertically, my arms and legs flailing uncontrollably. I could feel wind. Then I thought, "I don't want to travel; I just want to be there." Instantly I found myself in my mom's closet. For a moment, I was not sure where I was, or why, because everything looked weird, like it was illuminated from within, with its own light source. As I took a look around, I finally recognized her closet. I hadn't been there in 20 years. I noted that she had sweaters on hangars - not wise, because of course you know that hangars stretch funny little corners on the shoulders. She taught me that. I thought, "What am I doing in the closet?" Instantly I was back in my body waking up.

I picked up the phone and called my mom and said, "I just had an out-of-body experience and need to ask you if you have sweaters on hangars?" It was funny; she did not even question that I had just been in her closet. Her first comment was to defend her decision: "There was not enough room in the drawers!" Then I found out why I had arrived in her closet of all places. She wanted to show it to me, because she was so pleased that my sister had just helped her organize it. It was really awesome to be validated. It would be cool if everyone could have this kind of experience.

25 ∞ Prophecy

A prophecy, premonition or precognition gives you knowledge of some future event. It can come in a dream or in various waking forms. The way that you know that prophecy is foretelling the future, is that it has all the data of physical reality, but it hasn't happened yet. Sometimes prophecy revealed in dreams can come symbolically. It may not make logical sequential sense. For example, the characters are older, or there is something out of chronological order. There may be unfamiliar technology. There is also an intangible knowing that it is a different time. I have often felt a pressing doom accompanying prophetic dreams and visions.

Precognitive dreams are concretely validated when they eventually happen. Analysis between the premonitions and the eventual events as they unfold, reveals that some of the information that comes through is exact, and some of the information is symbolic. That makes it very tricky for relying on the details foretold, not to mention the mutability of events due to the conscious application of free will. For me, that makes me really timid about saying them out loud and on the record, but I know they won't ever be recognized as a phenomenon unless they are documented before they happen. Another challenge in relying on prophecy is that all time exists simultaneously, and there is a feedback system that takes into account energy input from all sources. Simply learning about what might potentially happen may affect the outcome in unpredictable ways. There are many ripples of causality that go out from any event.

The future is mutable, and even if we receive enough of the data, it is only one of the probabilities of what may come. It can be changed, and it can remain the same. I have experienced both premonitions that did come true and precognition of events that I was able to take action and prevent. Whether we have the ability to change what we have received in a predictive vision or dream, depends on many factors. I do not know what all of those factors are, but one seems to be whether you get enough information to make a change.

Often the knowledge comes symbolically, and you won't even recognize it as a premonition until you are in the midst of it, or after the fact, and therefore you would not be able to change it. In that case, the question would be, "Why were you given that information in the first place?" It could be as part of your training in understanding and discerning prophetic information. There is also some measure of comfort from knowing a particular event was in perfect Divine timing.

Fate Averted

I had a dream which I did not know was prophetic, although it was particularly vivid and stuck crisply in my memory. Because it was a bathroom dream, I just dismissed it as one of the thousands of dreams triggered by needing to go to the bathroom while I sleep.

Months later, I was on a trip in the car with my sisters and nephew. My nephew and I both needed a pit stop. We stopped at a fast food place and there was a long line of people waiting.

So we went to a gas station, but the restroom was out of order. As we were leaving, I noted the clerk was a nice young man from India. That might not be unusual in Southern California, but it was not as common in rural Ohio. As I noticed him, I suddenly remembered that I had dreamed this day!

In the dream, we are in a park setting, and my nephew and I go off to find a restroom. We get separated from the rest of the group, and all parties spend the remainder of the evening lost, worried, and annoyed.

So in real life, when we did get to the park and find the restroom - and the rest of the group wanted to separate and catch up later - I insisted that they wait for us. Although they might have been annoyed for a few minutes, we all had a great, relaxed, joyous day together. I felt blessed to have enough of the information I needed to significantly change the outcome of the events that I had seen in the prophetic dream.

26 ∞ Past Lives

In a memory, you have a lot of reality information. Past life memory feels just like a this-life memory. It will have the data of physical reality, except it will not be from the present body.

The way that I can determine that a past life is a memory, and not imagination or just a regular dream, is by thinking about all the detail present in the experience and analyzing the information. In a past life memory you experience all of the physical sensory data. For example, you remember the sound of your footsteps on the sidewalk.

Who Was I?

I have this one very clear memory where I was a Native American boy. I was tracking through a mountain where there was snow on the ground. It was soft snow covered by a thin layer of ice. I was being very careful to step on hard surfaces so that I didn't' leave any tracks. I could smell the snow - that crispness in the air. I just knew all of this reality data. I was aware of my position on the mountain, but I was also aware of my position on the planet.

All of my past life memories have the information of where I am on the planet, sort of like an internal GPS system. I can smell it. I can taste it. I can feel the gravity. I can feel myself in the body. In past life memories, I usually know what I look like, because I have seen myself at some point in those lives. I know my name - for example, as the Lokota youth, my name was Pūh-ōh-ūh-əh. I have a data set of identity, like all the stuff you know about yourself when you wake up in the morning.

As I discovered in my exploration of the levels of heaven, we are all one soul, in one eternal moment anyway, pretty much we can do individuation any which way we want. So my theory and my feeling for past lives is, once we individuate we can keep that individuation through several lifetimes. Returning to unity consciousness doesn't necessarily eliminate our individuation/identity along the same line. We can also just return to unity consciousness and not individuate anymore. It's our choice, we have that option available.

27 ∞ Confessions of a Doomtard

Bring on the Dooooom! I seem to be nearing the end of my doomtard phase. Probably influenced greatly by Revelations, stories of Armageddon, and the end of days, I have been fascinated by prophecies of the end of the world.. I have probably watched every doom-laden Sci-Fi feature and TV show. For the record, I don't ever actually wish harm on anyone. It wasn't until very recently, that I even examined myself to wonder why doom fascinates me and so many others. Since I am not an eschatologist or sociologist, I won't speak for others, but I did come to an understanding of some of the reasons that I personally find it so fascinating.

I have many prophetic dreams that have come true, in whole or in part - too many to count. I dreamed many of the details surrounding my mother's passing, although not the transition itself. That dream, which came 5 years before the event, included my nephew, who had not yet been conceived.

I also had two dreams of the meteorite that came down in Russia. The first time I saw it just like you see it on one of the videos, streaking across the sky. I was standing in front of a building. There was a very strong one-directional wind that knocked me over. It is also interesting to note that my point of view in the dream was that of the person in Russia, rather than the me who watched the YouTube video. In the second dream of the meteorite, I received the information that it would hit on the date of the closest approach of the next JPL-reported Near Earth Object. Although it was not the object from the JPL database, it did hit on that exact same day.

You can see even from these 2 examples that some of the information is exact. However, some details are vague, not included, or may even be symbolic. Needless to say, a few correct predictions would make anyone fascinated with doom, and I was certainly hooked.

I also dreamed of the earth's magnetic pole shift. Many of the elements in that dream have happened, like a slow drip across time. It's also possible that the pole shift in the dream was symbolic for the sun's magnetic pole shift, which was a process that unfolded from 2012 to 2014, much slower than previous solar magnetic pole flips. The important part of my dream was that the pole shift was a non-event, meaning it was not a big deal, and there was to be no great loss or damage from it.

For me there is a deeper symbolic element to this mega death, and that is the destruction of ego. I believe at some very deep level, that while the ego helps our physical self survive, it is also a hindrance to our spiritual awakening to our true self. Throughout the ages, in some religions, a death ritual has been performed before the resurrection of an awakened or enlightened being. The fascination with doom is the same kind of ritual death of ego within the collective consciousness.

That's ultimately good news for us if only an ego death occurs. This allows a spiritual awakening and rebirth in place of the prior ego-laden being. This does not have to be a complete release, just an expansion of consciousness beyond our former understanding of self.

When we know with certainty, that physical death is not the end of us, but the beginning of a magnificent experience in the afterlife, then physical death is not such a tragic event for the person dying. It is undeniably tragic for the family and friends who feel the loss. I have the deepest compassion for those who suffer with the death of a loved one.

Near death experiences show us that death is a release of ego, when the individual transcends the current reality consciousness and knows absolutely that there is more.

28 ∞ Unfolding the Experience

I was blessed that the first person I shared my story with was someone who had already had an out of body experience, and even though this kind of thing scared her, she believed me. Then I told my sister and she believed me too. Some of my family may not have believed me, but at least they were nice enough not to be mean to my face.

I was in a curious state of absolutely knowing it is true, and still wanting validation.

For many years after my enlightenment experience in the car, I assumed the love particle field information was already known by science. One day I was reading about a Nobel Prize winner in physics, and from what I read, it seemed he did not know about the structure and behavior of this field. That is when I finally realized that what I had experienced might be new information.

I decided to go back to college. I was going to major in physics, but I was too far behind in the math requirements to go straight to physics classes. However, I did take astronomy. The head of the department recommended that I join the local astronomers and astrophysics group. The group met monthly to watch university level physics courses together. A physicist attended who answered my many questions. So I got a crash course in physics without the tests. It was great.

My purpose for learning physics was to figure out what to call the experience I had. That was finally being satisfied through the physics group. As mentioned before, the closest physics term for what I experienced is probably the Higgs field, also called dark energy and dark matter. The term dark in this context has nothing to do with the darkness of the Vast Void, or even black holes. Physicists use the word dark because they don't know what it is. They are "in the dark" as to why there is matter and energy that they cannot perceive. The dark matter is inferred, because there is a much greater gravitational effect than can be accounted for by ordinary matter. Dark energy is inferred from the calculation of all the energy in the universe. Taking into consideration all the known matter and energy, it falls short of the expected energy (5% known, 20% dark matter, 75% dark energy estimates as of this writing).

In physics, there is this famous double slit experiment. When light is sent toward a solid surface with 2 open slits, and a photo sensitive material is on the other side, an interference pattern results that would be expected from a wave, not a particle. Scientists say that they don't understand why there is an interference pattern, if the nature of a photon is a physical particle. It should enter one slit or the other if one photon enters at a time. So, what is causing the interference?

Conversely, if the basic nature of photons and protons is a wave, then how and why do the results change when the observation is made to determine which slit the particle enters? The field that I have experienced, could explain the interference pattern. It could explain the fact that somehow the field is conscious and knows whether the particle is being observed or not. Assuming the field exists the way I have described it, there are several variations of that experiment that could validate the structure and behavior of the field.

29 ∞ Why Me?

Why me? Why not me? Who better than someone who doesn't have an education in math and physics to give the secret of the foundation of the physical universe as a way of saying, "See, I really do exist."

The biggest risk God took (not that God risks anything) in gracing me with this experience is that someone as deathly shy as I am might never be brave enough to share it.

Maybe because I asked for it, prayed for it, planned for it, wanted it, intended it, was open to it, was feeling my emotions and being in the present moment. Maybe it was because I felt such physical pain, I thought I might literally die of heartbreak. Maybe it was because I let go of every preconceived idea I had about the past, the future, what was possible, and who I am. I let go, opened up and did an emotional free fall without any safety apparatus.

I have asked this question many times, and finally I have to accept that I don't know what the special formula was. All I can do is share what I do know and hope it has value for others.

My hope is, that through my story, others can feel something as well. A large part of my personal motivation is that I want to do what I came here to do, so that I can go home well.

When the Divine Oneself touched me, there was this feeling of pure love blasting out of me. I felt there must be a way to share it with others. Usually when I do share, I feel reconnected, almost like the easiest path for me to divine love is directly through sharing my story with other people.

Another reason I want to get out there and share is so that I can validate your experience. We all will do well to validate each other, so that more and more people have the courage to share.

With more stories and experiences being shared, we add to the consensus of perception, and a new paradigm can be established.

30 ∞ Thoughts

God really exists. There really are angels and demons, and heaven and something like hell.

It really does matter how we live our lives. The thing is to live in love and be our best version of ourselves!

Let's love ourselves even as we feel we can do better. The motivation to do better is our own. The only judgment will always be our own, and is an exercise of our free will. God loves us and will welcome us home.

We can love ourselves. We can forgive ourselves. We can heal ourselves.

The point of life is the joy and adventure of the experience. The deeper and more intensely we live our experiences, the better. We are awakening to what we have been creating in our lives. Now we can begin to create more consciously and come to a place where we can be more responsible for what we create. We can understand that by being present, we have leverage to respond better to the life around us. We can be courageous in creating the life we choose to create. This feeling inside our hearts is our compass for our life purpose.

However difficult the struggle, we owe it to ourselves to strive to find the love, to find the truth and find our truest selves, to trust our hearts, and to forgive ourselves and others.

Imagine the impossible! Imagine we can all experience God's love directly, in our lifetime, without dying! Imagine a life without feeling the loss of loved ones who have passed, because our relationships actually continue! Imagine having the courage to face our transition from the physical, like the move to a new location. Imagine a society of individuals, that deeply understands the implications of the truth, that we are all one soul!

Because we truly understand that literally, what we do to our neighbor, we are doing to ourselves. So we love them and love ourselves. Imagine a world where we really loved all of our neighbors! Imagine having the courage to live our best lives.

Love the divine child that you are. Feel in your heart that you are Loved! Because you are Loved!

Helpful Books

Aczel, Amir D. The Mystery of the Aleph: Mathematics, the Kabbalah, and the Search for Infinity. New York: Four Walls Eight Windows, 2000. Print.

Bennett, David. *Voyage of Purpose*. N.p.: Findhorn, 2011. Print.

DeWitt Maltby, Deidre. While I Was Out... My Near Death Experience & Soul Altering Journey. N.p.: Xlibris, 2012. Print.

Drosnin, Michael, and Doron Vitstum. *The Bible Code*. New York: Simon & Schuster, 1997. Print.

Eisenman, Robert H., and Michael Owen Wise. The Dead Sea Scrolls Uncovered: The First Complete Translation and Interpretation of 50 Key Documents Withheld for over 35 Years. Shaftesbury, Dorset: Element, 1992. Print.

Filippenko, Alex. *Understanding the Universe: An Introduction to Astronomy*. Springfield, VA: Teaching Partnership, 1998. Print.

Robinson, James M. The Nag Hammadi Library The Definitive Translation of the Gnostic Scriptures. San Francisco, Ca: Harper, 1988. Print.

Sharp, Kimberly Clark. After the Light: What I Discovered on the Other Side of Life That Can Change Your World. New York: Author's Choice, 2003. Print.

Snelling, John. The Buddhist Handbook: The Complete Guide to Buddhist Schools, Teaching, Practice, and History. Rochester, VT: Inner Traditions, 1998. Print.

Suzuki, Daisetz Teitaro. *Zen and Japanese Culture*. London: Routledge and Kegan Paul, 1959. Print.

Taylor, Albert. Soul Traveler: A Guide to Out-of-body Experiences and the Wonders beyond. New York: Dutton, 1998. Print.

Zukav, Gary. *The Seat of the Soul*. New York: Fireside Simon and Schuster, 1990. Print.

facebook.com/authormarydeioma

youtube.com/user/mdeioma

Made in the USA
San Bernardino, CA
09 May 2015